GRADE-3 MEASUREMENT AND DATA HANDLING

Fun-filled Activities

Om KIDZ

An imprint of Om Books International

Measuring Length

Look at the figures. Circle the best estimate for each length.

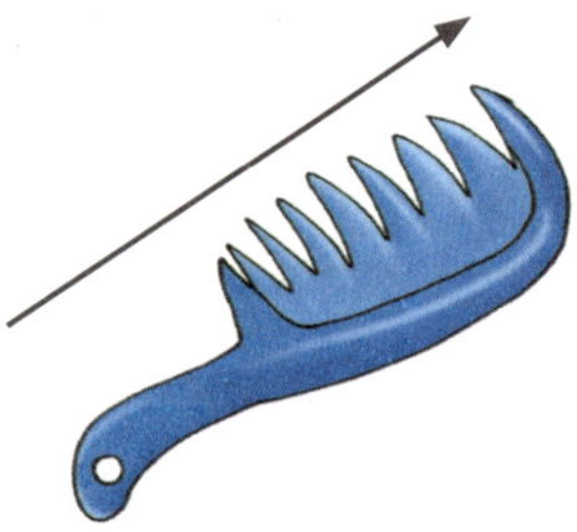

A. unicycle	5 cm	12 cm	20 cm
B. teddy bear	8 cm	14 cm	4 cm
C. robe	12 cm	18 cm	11 cm
D. comb	3 cm	4 cm	7 cm
E. leaf	5 cm	4 cm	8 cm

CHALLENGE

Measure the actual length of the objects indicated above. How much does it differ from your estimation?

Conversion Of Units

The standard unit of measuring length according to the metric system is metre (m). Other units are millimetre (mm), centimetre (cm) and kilometre (km).

To change centimetres to millimetres, multiply by 10.

1 cm = mm x 10

5 cm	=	50 mm
6 cm	=	60 mm
12 cm	=	120 mm

To change metres to centimetres, multiply by 100.

1 m = cm x 100

5 m	=	500 cm
6 m	=	600 cm
12 m	=	1200 cm

To change kilometres to metres, multiply by 1000.

1km = m X 1000

5 km	=	5000 m
6 km	=	6000 m
12 km	=	12000 m

To change metres into kilometres and centimetres into metres:

km X 1000 ← m X 100 ← cm

5 km	5000 m	5,00,000 cm
6 km	6000 m	6,00,000 cm
12 km	12000 m	12,00,000 cm

Converting Kilometres Into Metres

Convert the units from kilometres to metres. The first one has been done for you.

8 km 1 km = 1000 m 8 km = 8 x 1000 m = 8000 m	6 km
10 km	5 km
13 km	9 km

CHALLENGE

What is the distance in kilometres between your school and house? What is the easiest way to know this without actual measurement?

Converting Metres Into Kilometres

To convert metres to kilometres, simply divide the number by 1000.

9000 metres =

9000 ÷ 1000 = 9 m

Convert the units from metres to kilometres.

a. 9000 m

b. 17000 m

c. 7000 m

d. 8000 m

e. 14000 m

f. 3000 m

QUICK TIP

To change numbers like 8100 m to kilometres just write the digit at thousands place as kilometres and the rest of the digits as metres. Example: 8100 m = 8 km, 100 m

Converting Metres Into Centimetres

To convert metres to centimetres, follow these steps:

1 m = 100 cm

5 m = 5 X 100= 500 cm

To convert 5 m 40 cm to metres.

5 m = 5 X 100

= 500 cm

So, 5 m 40 cm= 500 cm + 40 cm

= 540 cm

Convert these units into centimetres.

a. 7 m

b. 9 m

c. 6 m 88 cm

d. 1 m 50 cm

e. 5 m 60 cm

f. 4 m 100 cm

Converting Centimetres Into Metres

To convert centimetres to metres, divide by 100 or just remove two zeros at the end.

For example:

900 cm = 9 m

800 cm = 8 m

1000 cm = 10 m

CHALLENGE

Measure the length of a door in cms. Then convert the length into metres.

Convert these units into metre.

a. 700 cm

b. 400 cm

c. 900 cm

d. 3000 cm

e. 3700 cm

f. 800 cm

g. 600 cm

h. 500 cm

Measuring Mass

Look at the figures. Choose the best estimate for each mass.

700 grams
15 kilograms
10 kilograms

50 grams
500 grams
50 kilograms

5 grams
100 grams
2 kilograms

100 grams
350 grams
3 kilograms

TRY IT

Collect some objects and estimate their weight. Then measure their weight and make a comparison chart.

Conversion Of Units

The standard units for measuring mass are grams (g) and kilograms (kg).

1 kg= 1000 grams

To change kilograms into grams:

1 kg = 1000 grams
9 kg = 9 X 1000
= 9000 grams

To change grams into kilograms and vice versa:

g ÷ 1000 ⟶ 1kg

5000 g	⟶	5 kg
8000 g	⟶	8 kg
12000 g	⟶	12 kg

CHALLENGE

Are there any units that are larger than kilogram? Find out.
Make a conversion chart for this unit into kilograms and grams.

Converting Kilograms Into Grams

Convert the units from kilograms to grams.
One has been done for you.

6 kg
1 kg = 1000 g
6 kg = 6 x 1000 g
= 6000 g

9 kg

8 kg

4 kg

7 kg

5 kg

3 kg

CHALLENGE

A box weighs 7 kg and another box weighs 3000 grams more than 4 kg. Which is heavier?

Converting Grams Into Kilograms

We know that:

1000 g = 1 kg

4000 g = 4 kg

4500 g = 4 kg 500 g

Convert the units from grams to kilograms.

a. 9000 g

b. 17000 g

c. 7000 g

d. 6000 g

e. 4000 g

f. 3000 g

g. 10000 g

h. 14000 g

CHALLENGE

Fill in the correct mass to balance the two sides given below.

2 kg 700 g + ______ = 2 kg 800 g

Conversion Of Mass

Convert 7 kg 600 g to grams

1 kg = 1000 g

7 kg = 7000 g

So, 7 kg 600 g = 7000 g + 600 g

= 7600 g

Convert the following into grams.

1. 5 kg 500 g
2. 9 kg 700 g
3. 4 kg 400 g
4. 8 kg 130 g
5. 3 kg 280 g
6. 1 kg 690 g

TRY IT

Subtract 2 kg 225 g from 4 kg 325 g. How much is left?

Measuring Capacity

We know that capacity is the amount that a container can hold.
The containers given below show the amount of liquid they can hold.

The standard unit of measuring capacity is litres (l) and millilitres (ml).

1)

2)

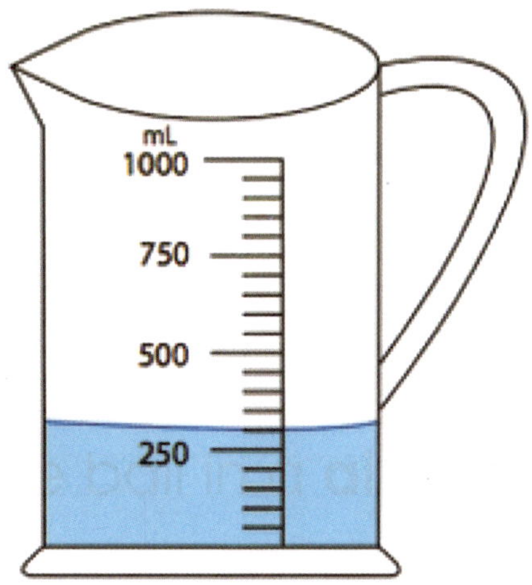

3)

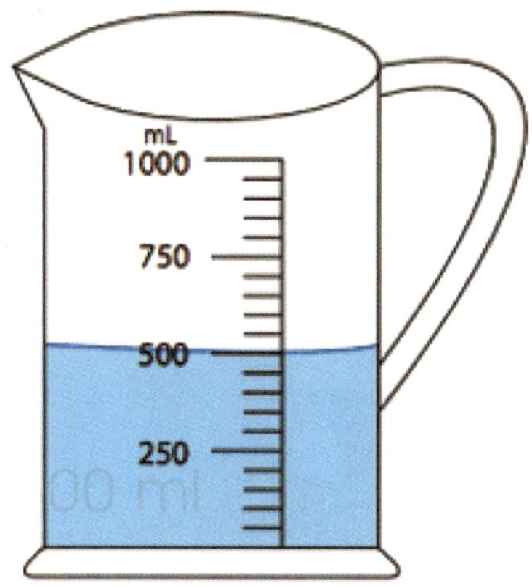

What capacity do you think these containers can hold? Write your estimate.

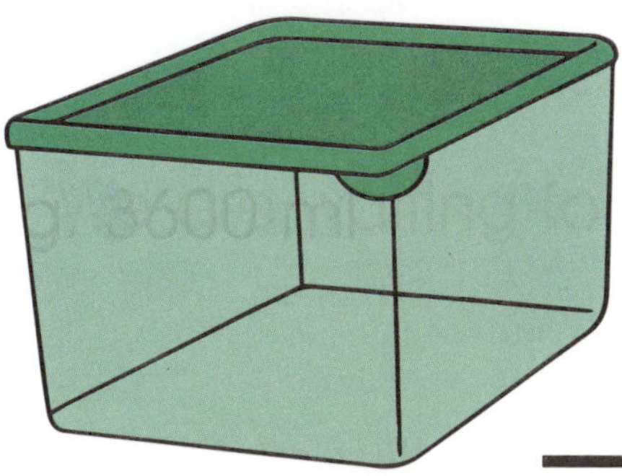

____

____

____

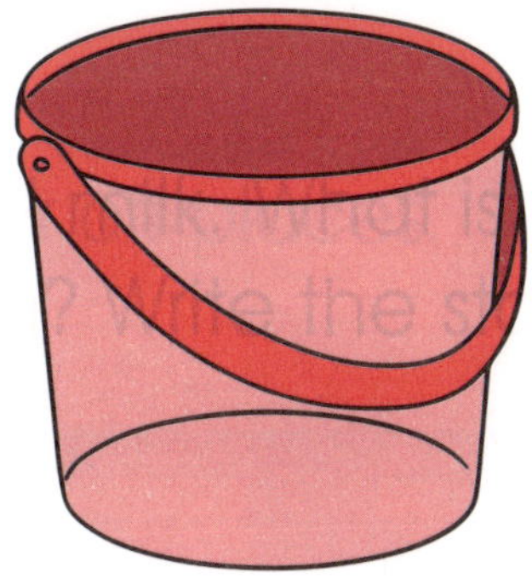

____

Converting Litres Into Millilitres

To convert litres into millilitres:

1 x 1000 = 1000 ml

8 litres = 8000 ml

To convert 8 l 600 ml:

8 X 1000 = 8000 ml

8 l 600 ml = 8000 ml + 600 ml

= 8600 ml

Convert these units into millilitres.

a. 5 l

b. 9 l

c. 6 l 550 ml

d. 3 l 400 ml

e. 7 l 690 ml

f. 8 l 700 ml

g. 5 l 750 ml

h. 4 l 702 ml

Converting Millilitres Into Litres

1000 ml = 1 l

6000 ml = 6 l

6800 ml = 6 l 800 ml

Convert the units from millilitres to litres.

a. 8000 ml

b. 27000 ml

c. 4500 ml

d. 7300 ml

e. 5900 ml

f. 9000 ml

g. 3600 ml

h. 4100 ml

CHALLENGE

Mix 1 l 300 ml water and 2 l 300 ml milk. What is the total quantity of the solution after mixing? Write the statement here.

Telling Time

Write the time shown by each clock on the lines below.

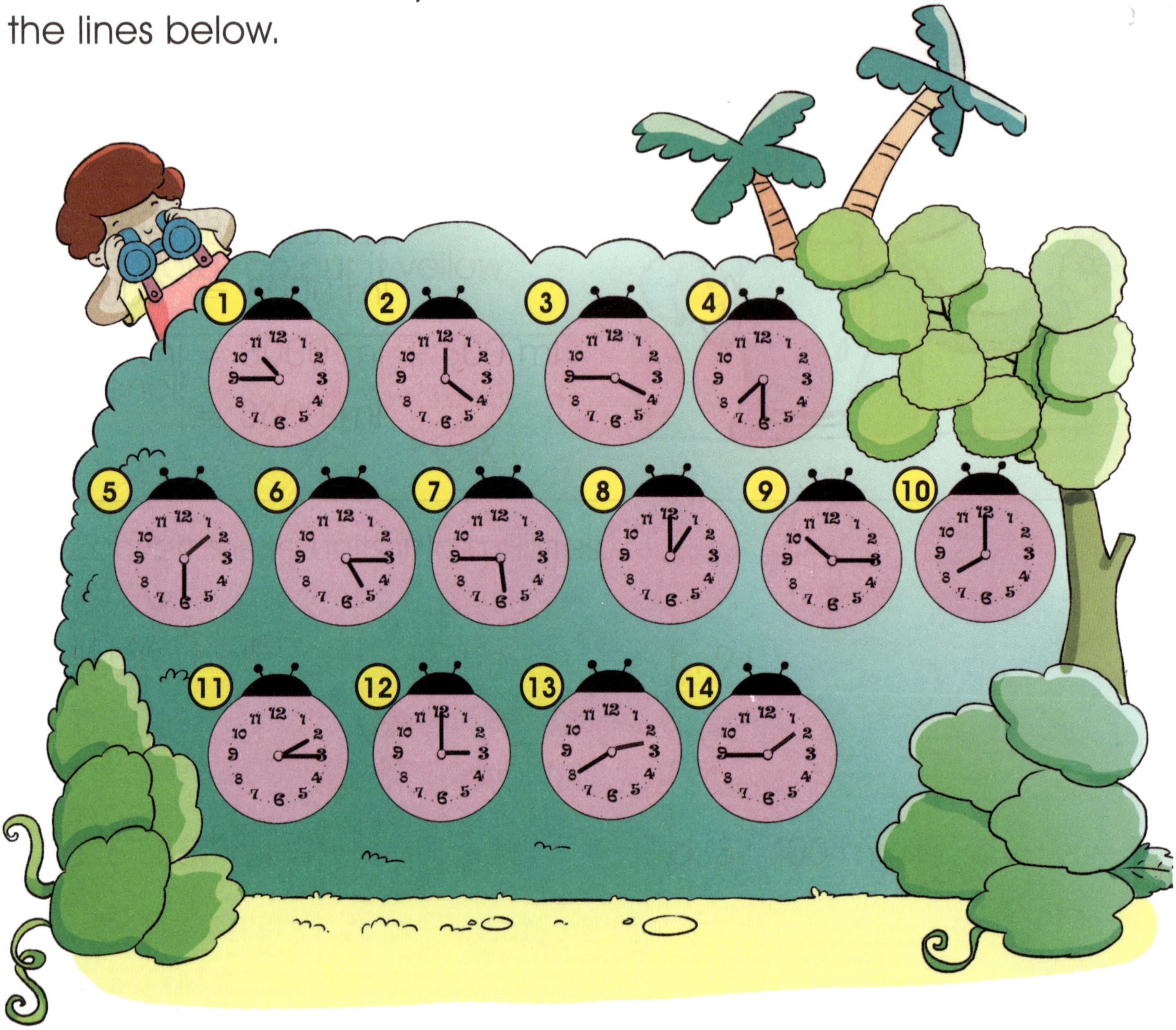

1. __________ 2. __________ 3. __________ 4. __________

5. __________ 6. __________ 7. __________ 8. __________

9. __________ 10. __________ 11. __________ 12. __________

13. __________ 14. __________

Conversion Of Time

We know that:

1 hour = 60 minutes

To convert hours into minutes, multiply the hours by 60.

For example:

3 hours = 3 X 60 = 180 minutes.

Convert the hours into minutes.

8 hours	6 hours
12 hours	14 hours
11 hours	10 hours

Converting Hours And Minutes Into Minutes

Let us see how to convert hours and minutes into minutes.

Convert 2 hours 30 minutes into minutes.

1 hour = 60 minutes

2 hours = 2 X 60 = 120 minutes

So, 2 hours 30 minutes

= 120 minutes + 30 minutes

= 150 minutes

Convert the given hours and minutes into minutes.

a. 6 hours 45 min	b. 4 hours 33 min
c. 9 hours 10 min	d. 3 hours 20 min
e. 5 hours 5 min	f. 2 hours 15 min
g. 7 hours 30 min	h. 1 hour 1 min

Converting Minutes Into Seconds

We know that:

1 minute = 60 seconds

So, to convert minutes into seconds, we multiply the minutes by 60.

2 minutes = 2 X 60 = 120 seconds

CHALLENGE

What time is it if the clock shows 5 hours more than 3 pm and the nearest hour is not 1 pm?

Convert the minutes into seconds.

8 minutes	12 minutes
7 minutes	15 minutes
22 minutes	31 minutes
40 minutes	50 minutes

Writing Time In 24-hour Clock

There are two ways of telling the time:

12-hour clock

24-hour clock

The 12-hour clock runs from 1am to 12 noon and then from 1pm to 12 midnight.

When we write time in the 24- hour clock, the hours start at zero and go through to 23. The last hour is written as 00:00

We usually write the 24-hour clock time in the hh:mm format, where h is the hour and m is the minute.

The minutes and seconds never change when changing between 24 hour and 12 hour times.

Examples:

14:36 = 2:36 pm

09:24 = 9:24 am

00:45 = 12:45 am

20:36 = 8:36 pm

02:12 = 2:12 am

17:48 = 5:48 pm

12:15 = 12:15 pm

23:56 = 11:56 pm

Conversion Of Time

To change the time from 12-hour to 24-hour, just add 12 to the hour, if the time is in pm. No changes are made for the time in am and 12 pm.

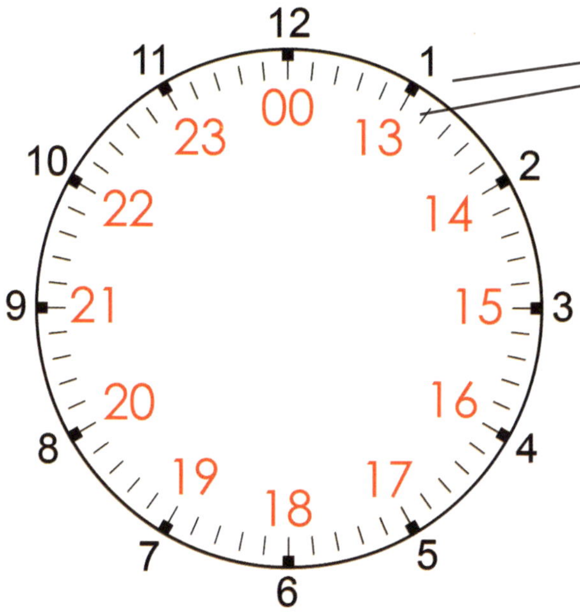

1:00 pm becomes 13:00 in 24-hour time format.

Convert these times into 24-hour clock times.

12-hour	24-hour
5:25 am	
10:20 pm	
11:35 am	
12:40 pm	
6:15 am	
1:33 am	
2:50 pm	
10:45 am	
12:00 noon	

12-hour	24-hour
6:13 am	
9:40 pm	
3:45 am	
11:20 pm	
9:10 am	
4:40 am	
7:50 pm	
12:45 am	
1:00 pm	

Conversion Of Time

Convert these 24-hour clock times to 12-hour clock time.

24-hour	12-hour
17:02	
09:39	
05:36	
12:11	
22:05	

24-hour	12-hour
18:53	
00:17	
02:30	
21:15	
23:45	

Draw the correct time on the clock faces to match the 24-hour clock time.

04:00

14:30

16:10

12:00

08:15

19:30

11:50

18:45

Reading A Pictograph

Paula and her friends painted eggs for Easter. Read the pictograph that shows how many eggs each one painted.

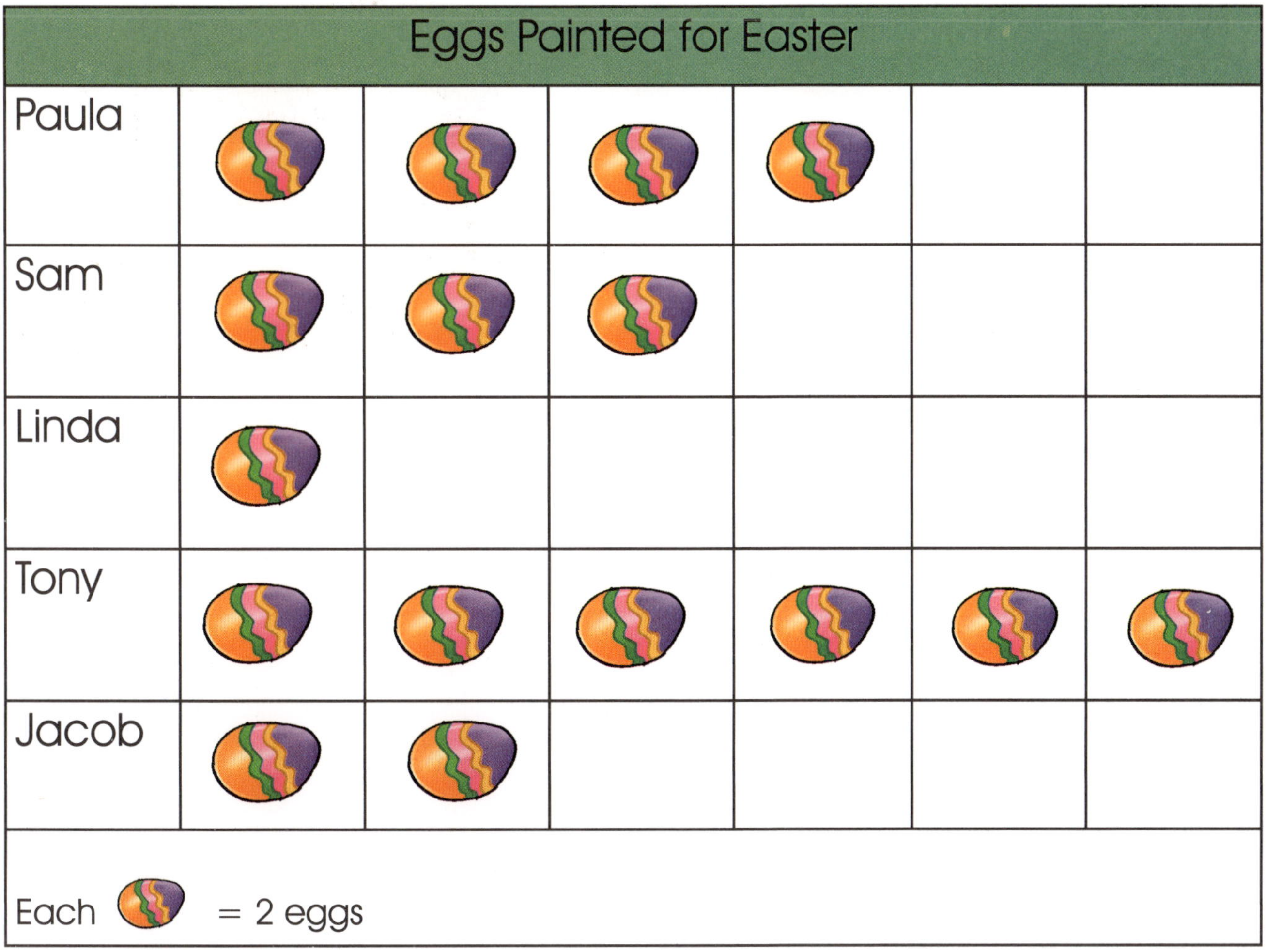

Answer the questions.

1. Who painted the most eggs? ______________________
2. Who painted the least eggs? ______________________
3. Who painted four eggs? ______________________
4. How many more eggs did Sam paint than Jacob? ______________________
5. Paula and Linda put their eggs in the basket. How many eggs do they have in all? ______________________

Completing A Pictograph

Use the information bank to complete the pictograph.
Each  represents one animal.

Information Bank			
cats	5	birds	4
dogs	6	rabbits	2
fish	3	turtles	1

Class Pets							
cats							
dogs							
fish							
birds							
rabbits							
turtles							

CHALLENGE

How will the pictograph change if 2 more pets are added to each kind. Draw a new pictograph in your notebook.

Using A Pictograph

Study the graph.

Visit to the Zoo	
mammals	★ ★ ★ ★
reptiles	★ ★
birds	★ ★ ★
amphibians	★
insects	★ ★

Key
1 ★ = 10 animals

Use the graph to solve these questions.

John sees 10 snakes and 5 turtles. How many other reptiles did he see? ____________

Maria sees 15 tigers. How many mammals are not tigers as per the graph? ____________

Tom sees 3 parrots and 8 pelicans. How many birds are not parrots and pelicans? ____________

Lara sees 7 butterflies. How many of the insects are not butterflies? ____________

How many less amphibians does the zoo have than reptiles?

____

How many birds and mammals are there in all?

____

Reading A Bar Graph

Use the graph to answer the questions.

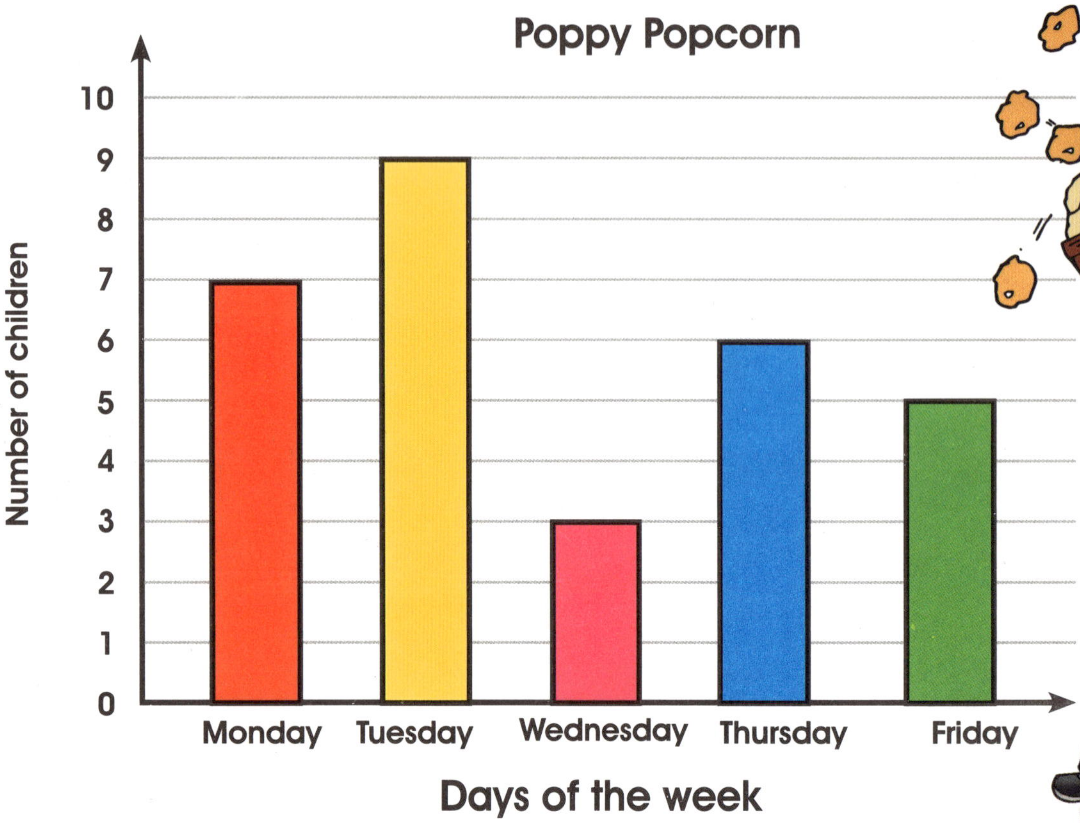

1. On which day was the most popcorn sold?

____

2. How many buckets of popcorn were sold on Thursday?

____

3. How many buckets of popcorn were sold on these 5 days?

____

4. How many more buckets of popcorn were sold on Tuesday than on Wednesday?

____

5. How will the bar graph change if 3 more children took popcorn on Monday?

____

Completing A Bar Graph

Use the race results to complete the bar graph.

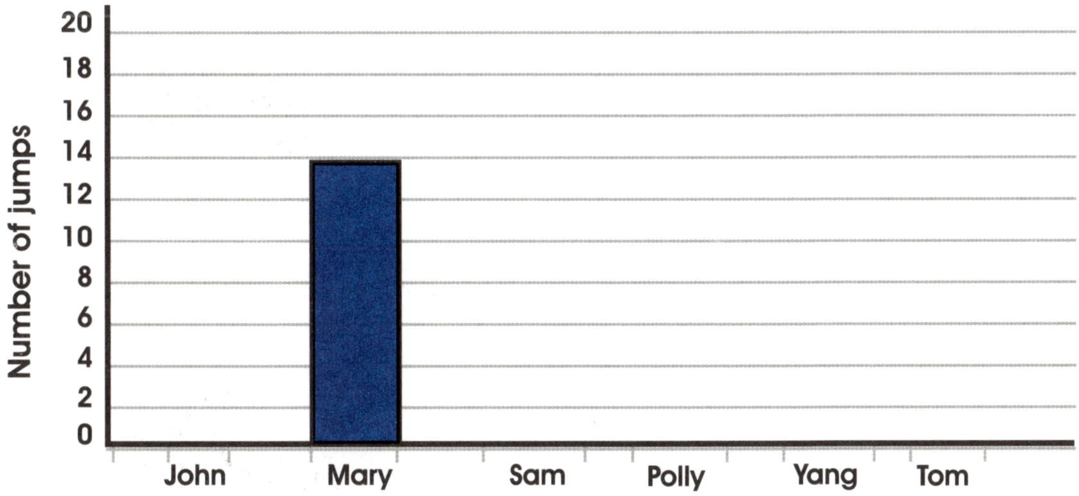

Answer these questions.

1. Who won the contest? ______________
2. Who had the least number of jumps?

   ____

3. Who had more jumps than John but not as many as Sam? ___________
4. How many more jumps did Tom have than Polly? ______________
5. How many jumps did Sam and Yang had together? ______________

John- 13	Polly- 8
Mary- 14	Yang- 10
Sam- 20	Tom- 16

Reading A Venn Diagram

The Venn diagram shows the scores of Lee, Linda and Neo in a dice game. Look carefully at it and answer the questions.

1. What are the scores that all three children scored? ________
2. What is the highest score among the three? ________
3. Find the total of Lee's scores. ________
4. Find the sum of Linda's score excluding Neo's score. ________
5. Find the difference between the highest score of Linda and lowest score of Neo. ________
6. Find the total of both Lee and Linda's score. ________

Making A Venn Diagram

Paul, Bob and Jim had a bubble blowing competition. Use the score table to make a Venn diagram for each round.

Paul	Bob	Jim
20, 32, 11, 16, 18	22, 32, 11, 17, 19	15, 22, 19, 18, 10

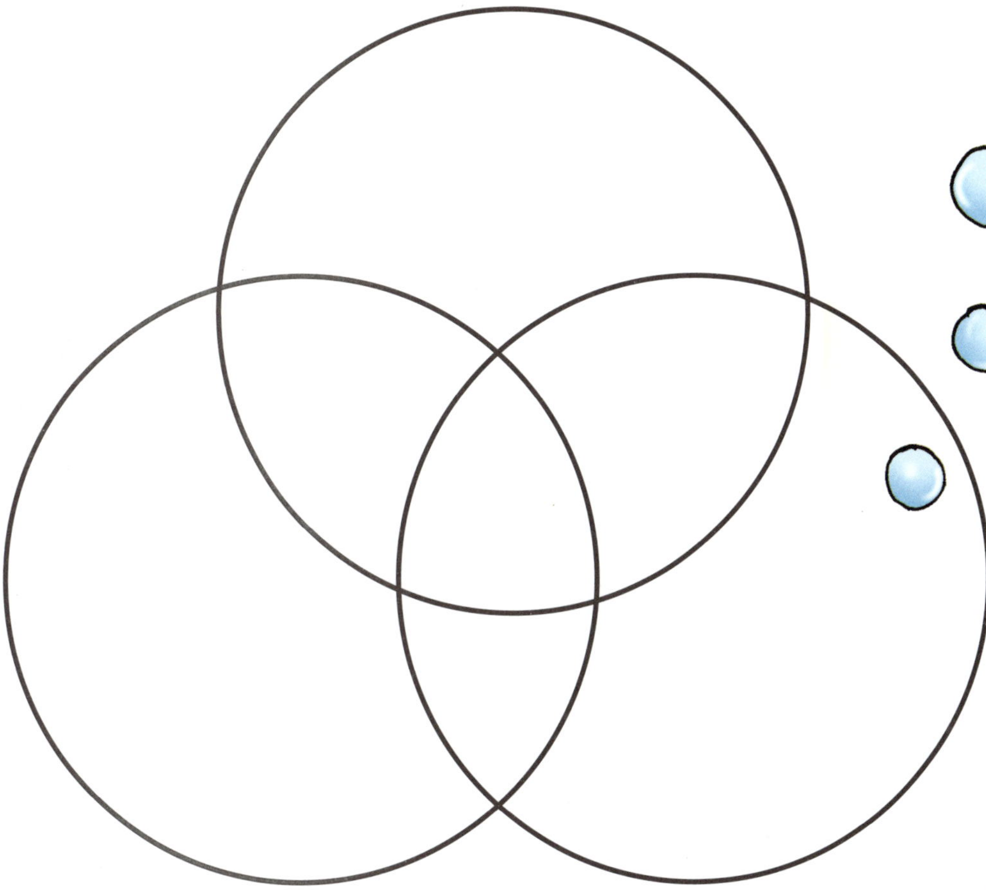

CHALLENGE

Ask your friends the marks they scored in English in the last assignment. Make a Venn diagram.

Answer Key

Page 2

Children will do on their own.
Answers may vary.

Page 4

b. 6 km = 6 x1000
= 6000 m

c. 10 km = 10 x1000
=10000 m

d. 5 km = 5 x1000
= 5000 m

e. 13 km = 13 x1000
= 13000 m

f. 9 km = 9 x1000
= 9000 m

Page 5

a. 9 km
b. 17 km
c. 7 km
d. 8 km
e. 14 km
f. 3 km

Page 6

a. 7 X 100 = 700 cm

b. 9 X 100 = 900 cm

c. 6 m 88 cm = 6 x 100 + 88 cm
= 600 + 88 = 688 cm

d. 1 m 50 cm = 1 x 100 + 50 cm
= 100 + 50 = 150 cm

e. 5 m 60 cm = 5 x 100 + 60 cm
= 500 + 60 = 560 cm

f. 4 m 100 cm = 4 x 100 + 100 cm
= 400 + 100 = 500 cm

Page 7

a. 7 m
b. 4 m
c. 9 m
d. 30 m
e. 37 m
f. 8 m
g. 6 m
h. 5 m

Page 8

Children will do on their own.

Page 10

a. 9 kg = 9000 g
b. 8 kg = 8000 g
c. 4 kg = 4000 g
d. 7 kg = 7000 g
e. 5 kg = 5000 g
f. 3 kg = 3000 g

Page 11

a. 9 kg
b. 17 kg
c. 7 kg
d. 6 kg
e. 4 kg
f. 3 kg
g. 10 kg
h. 14 kg

Page 12

a. 5500 g
b. 9700 g
c. 4400 g
d. 8130 g
e. 3280 g
f. 1690 g

Page 13

Children will do on their own.

Page 14

a. 5000 ml
b. 9000 ml
c. 6550 ml
d. 3400 ml
e. 7690 ml
f. 8700 ml
g. 5750 ml
h. 4702 ml

Page 15

a. 8 l
b. 27 l
c. 4 l 500 ml
d. 7 l 300 ml
e. 5 l 900 ml
f. 9 l
g. 3 l 600 ml
h. 4 l 100 ml

Page 16

1. 10: 45
2. 4:00
3. 3: 45
4. 7: 30
5. 1:30
6. 5: 15
7. 5:45
8. 1:00
9. 10:15
10. 8:00
11. 2:15
12. 3:00
13. 2:40
14. 1:45

Answer Key

Page 17

a. 480 min

b. 360 min

c. 720 min

d. 840 min

e. 660 min

f. 600 min

Page 18

a. 405 min

b. 273 min

c. 550 min

d. 200 min

e. 305 min

f. 135 min

g. 450 min

h. 61 min

Page 19

a. 480 sec

b. 720 sec

c. 420 sec

d. 900 sec

e. 1320 sec

f. 1860 sec

g. 2400 sec

h. 3000 sec

Page 21

1. 05:25
2. 22:20
3. 11:35
4. 12:40
5. 06:15
6. 01:33
7. 14:50
8. 10:45
9. 12:00
10. 06:13
11. 21:40
12. 03:45
13. 23:20
14. 09:10
15. 04:40
16. 19:50
17. 00:45
18. 13:00

Page 22

5:02 pm
9:39 am
5:36 am
12:11 pm
10:05 pm
6:53 pm
12:17 am
2:30 am
9:15 pm
11:45 pm

Page 23

1. Tony
2. Linda
3. Jacob
4. 2 eggs
5. 10 eggs

Page 24

Children will do on their own

Page 25

1. 5 reptiles
2. 25 mammals
3. 19 birds
4. 13 insects
5. 10 amphibians
6. 70 in all

Page 26

1. Tuesday
2. 6
3. 30 in all
4. 6 more buckets
5. The bar on Monday would read 10 and highest number of popcorn buckets would be sold on Monday then, not Tuesday.

Page 27

Children will make the graph on their own.

1. Sam
2. Polly
3. Mary and Tom
4. 8 jumps
5. 30 jumps

Answer Key

Page 28

1. 18 and 24
2. 30
3. 103
4. 27
5. 103 + 154 = 257

Page 29

Children will make the Venn diagram on their own.